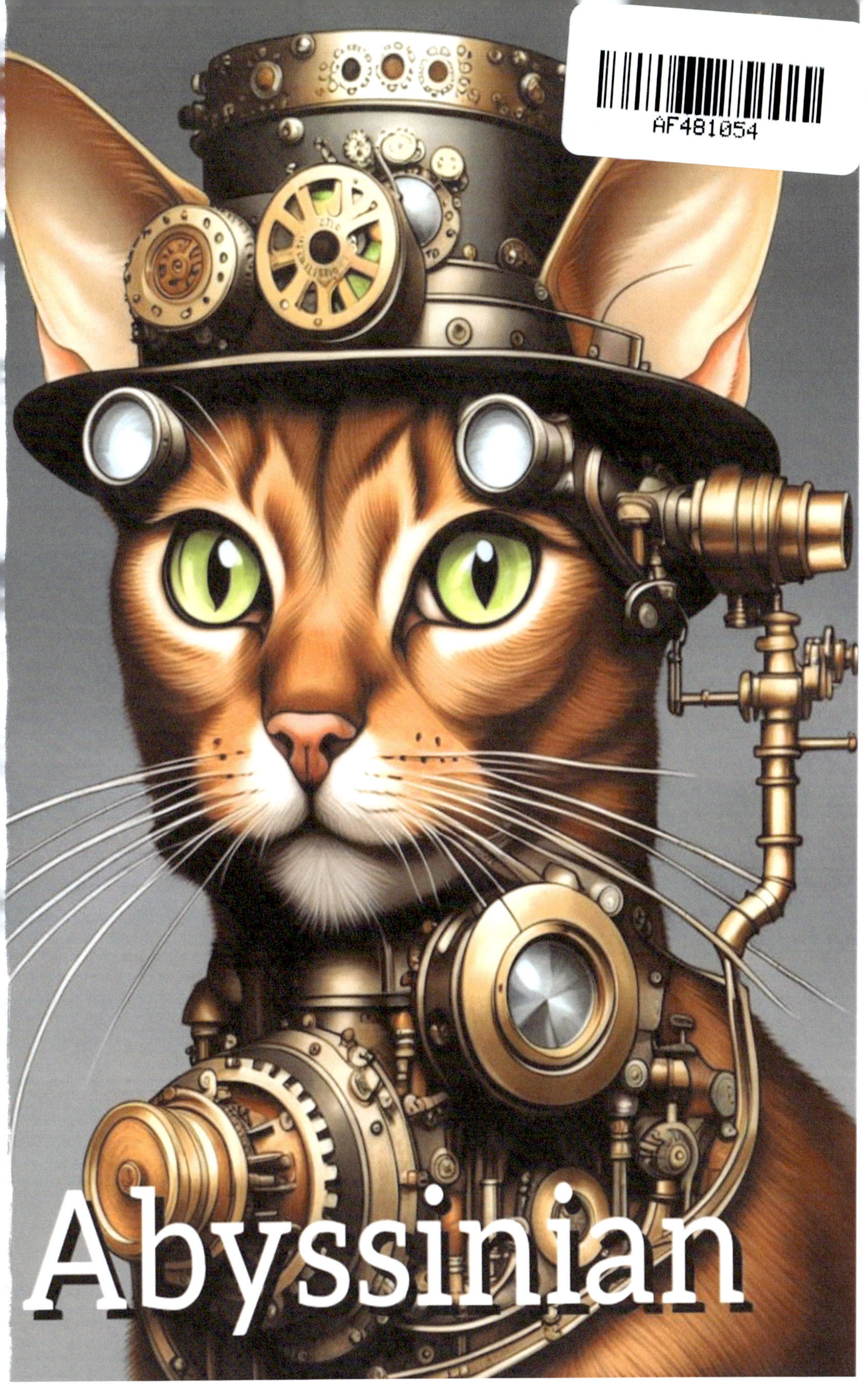

AF481054
Abyssinian

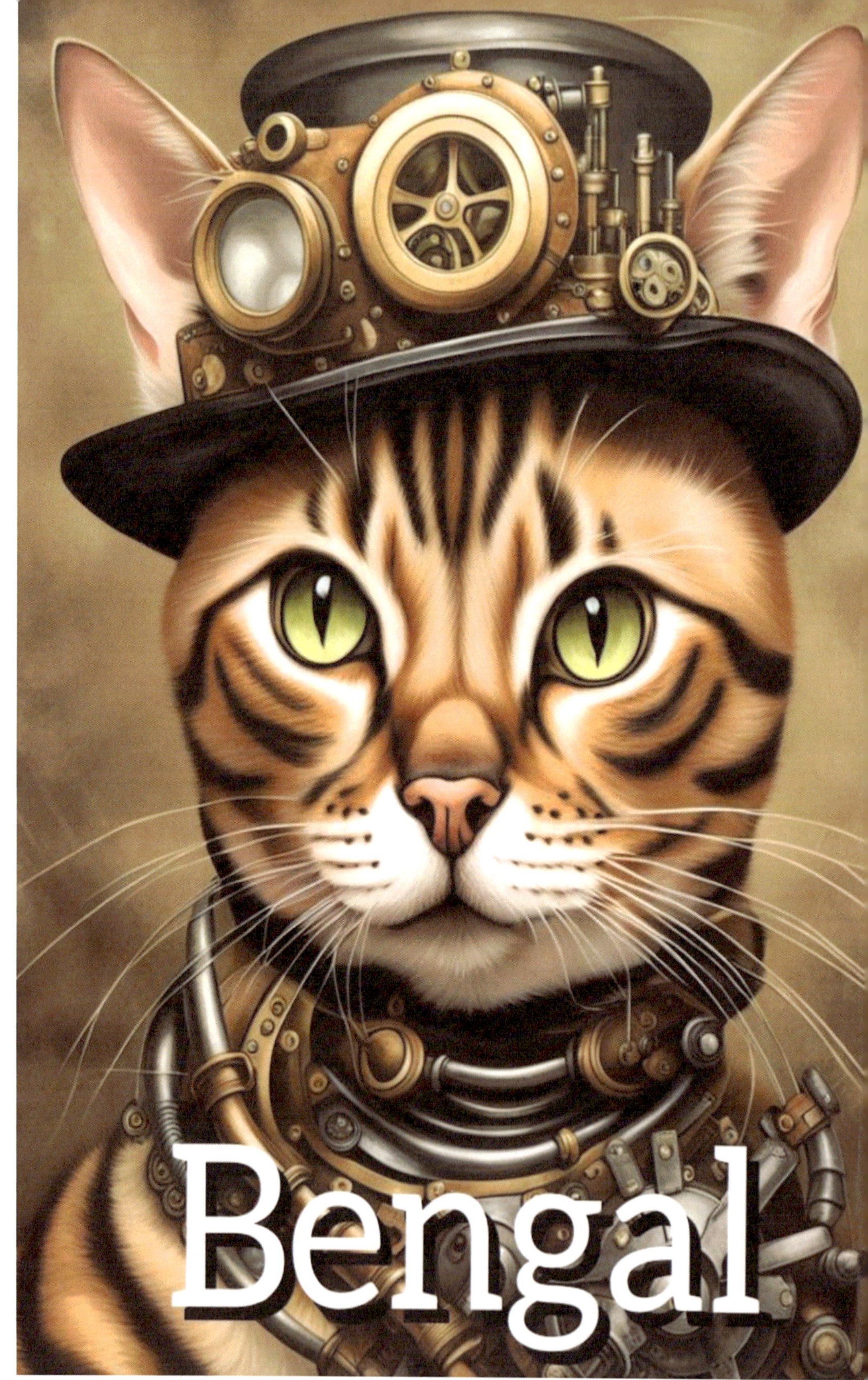
Bengal

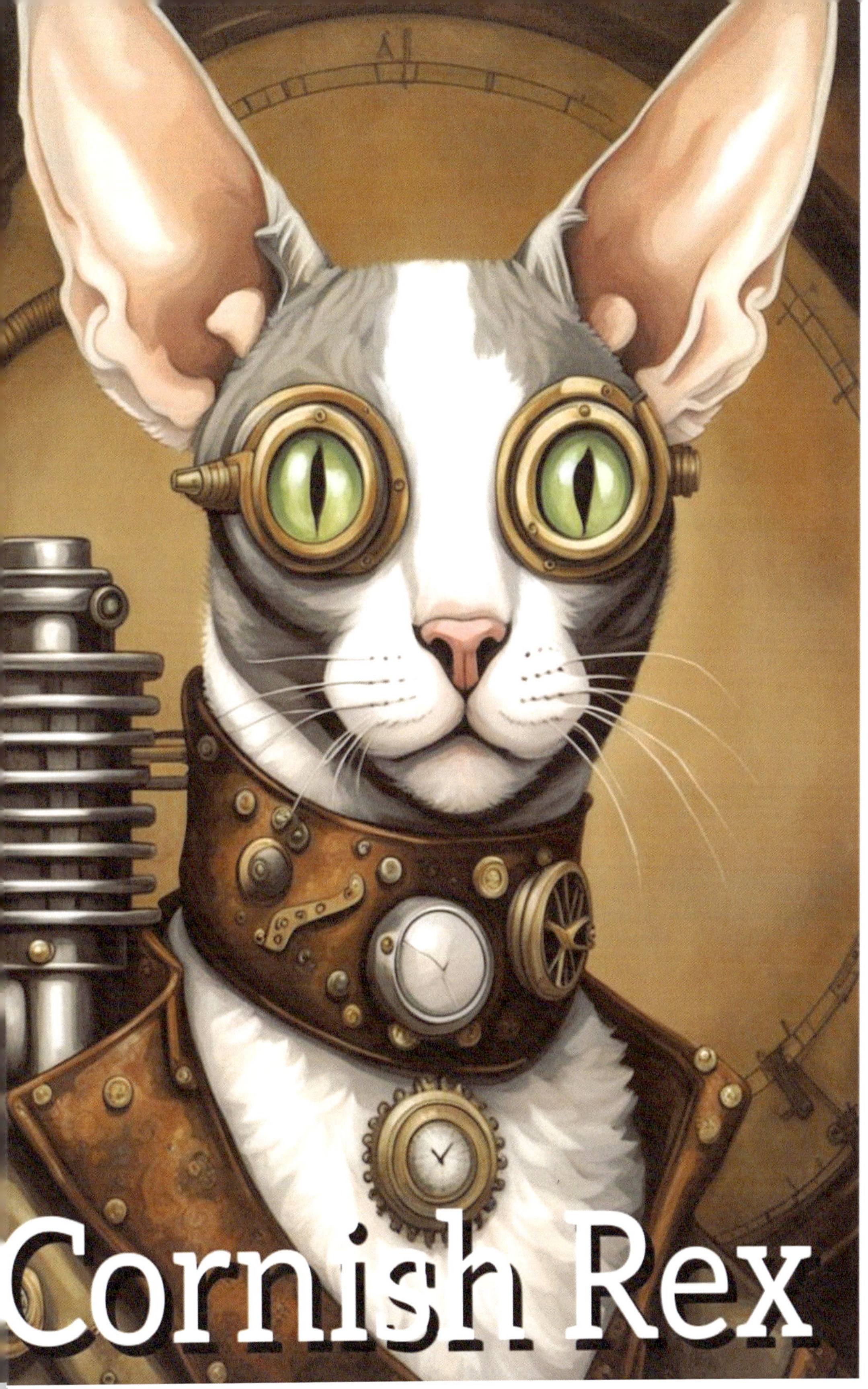

Cornish Rex

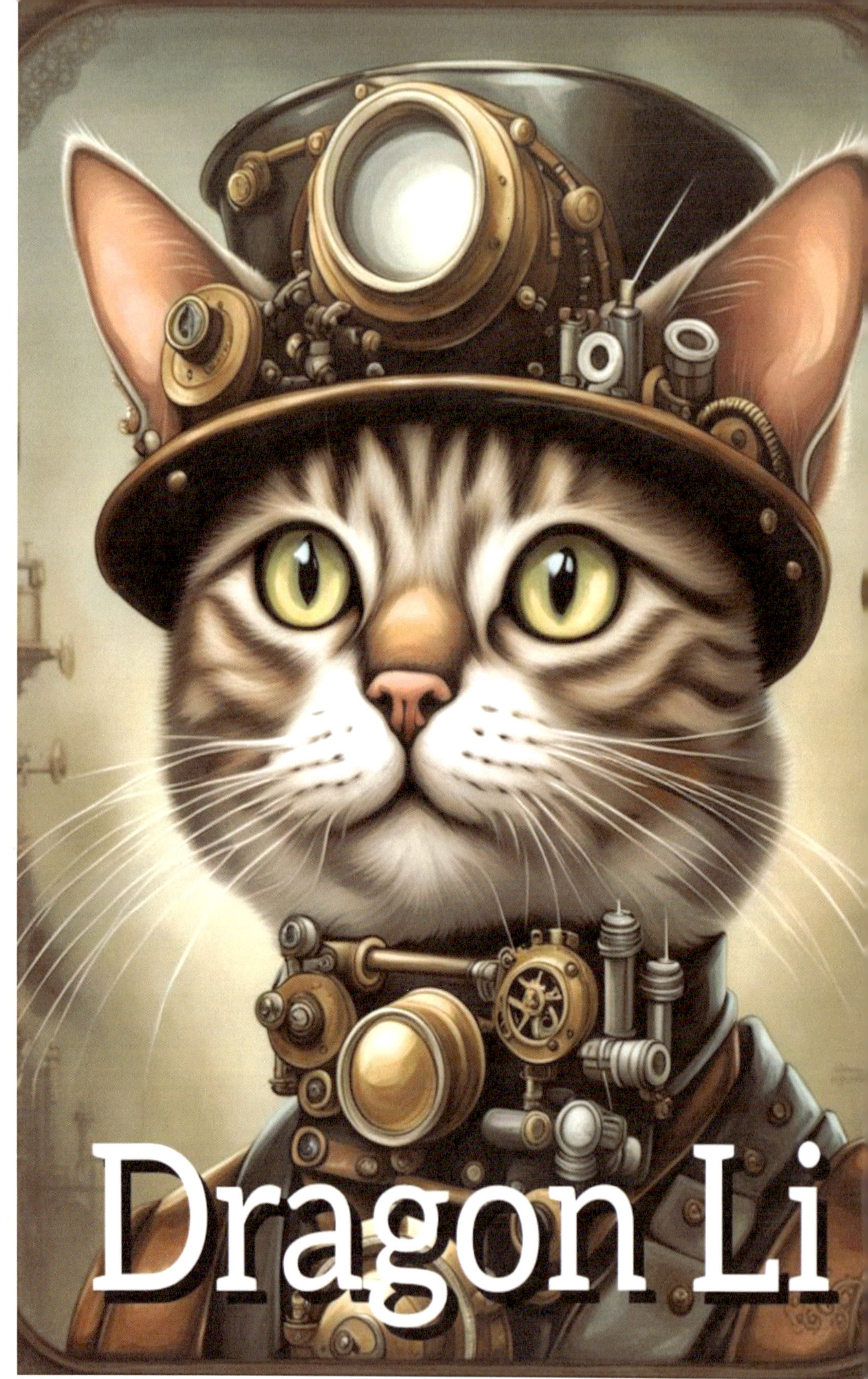
Dragon Li

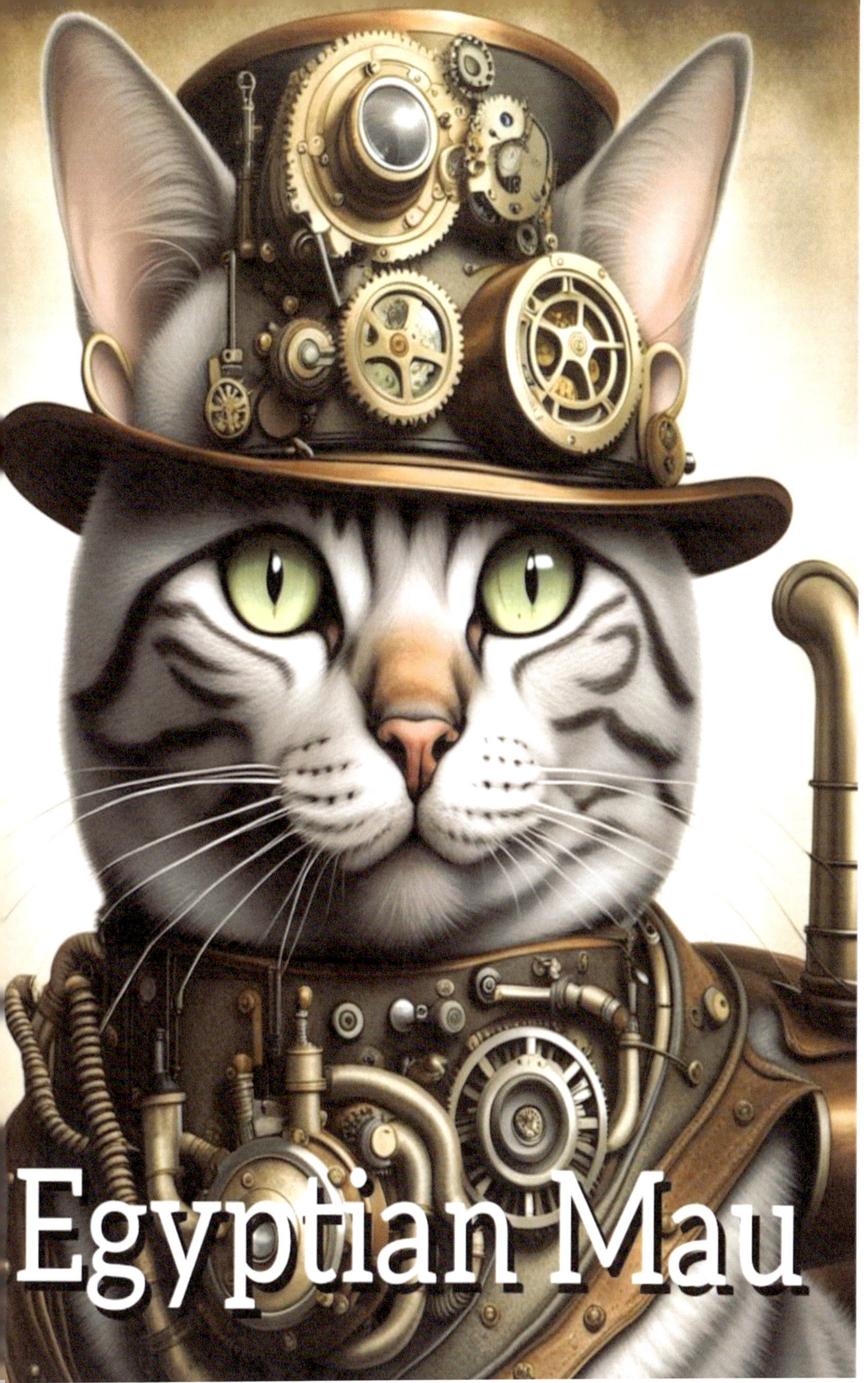
Egyptian Mau

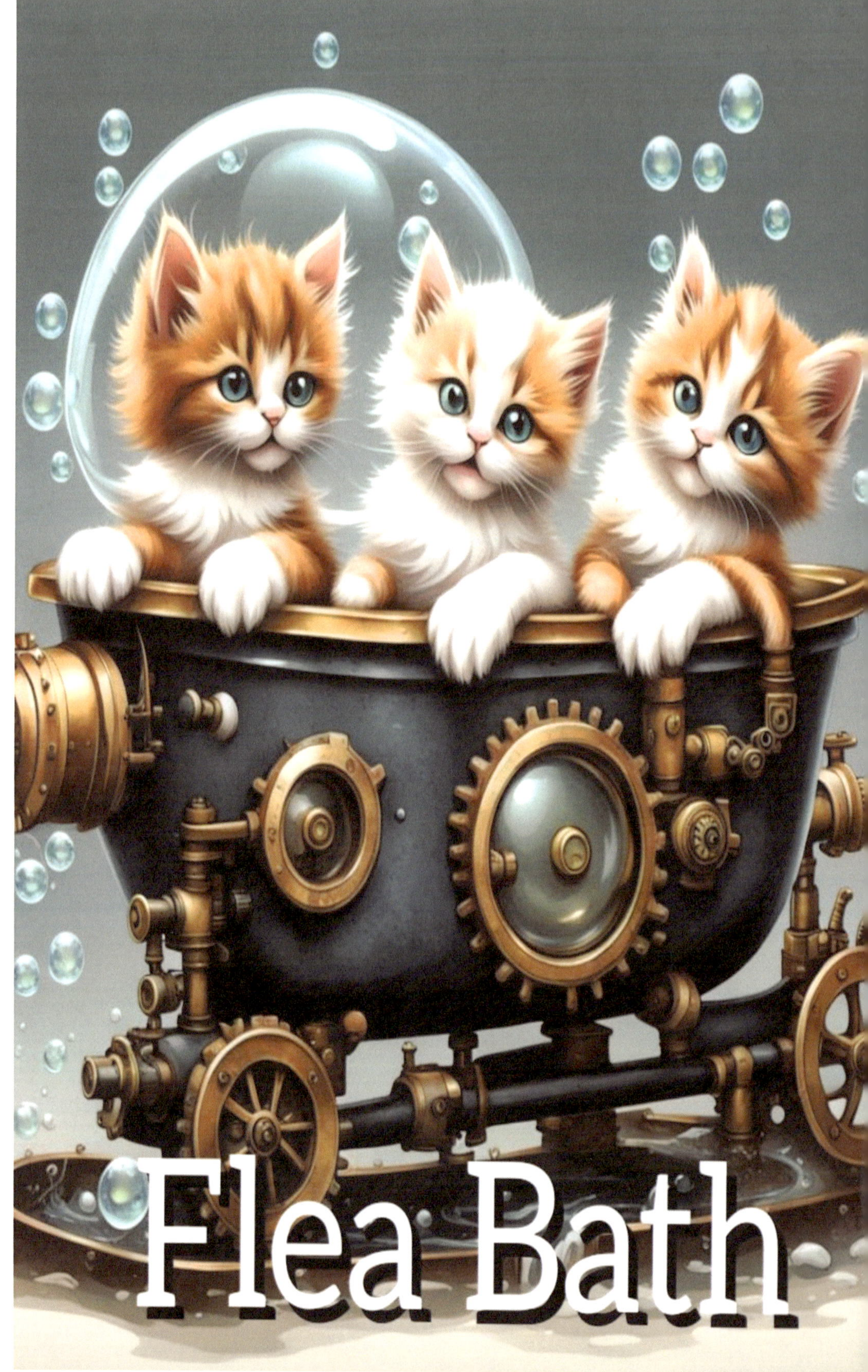

Flea Bath

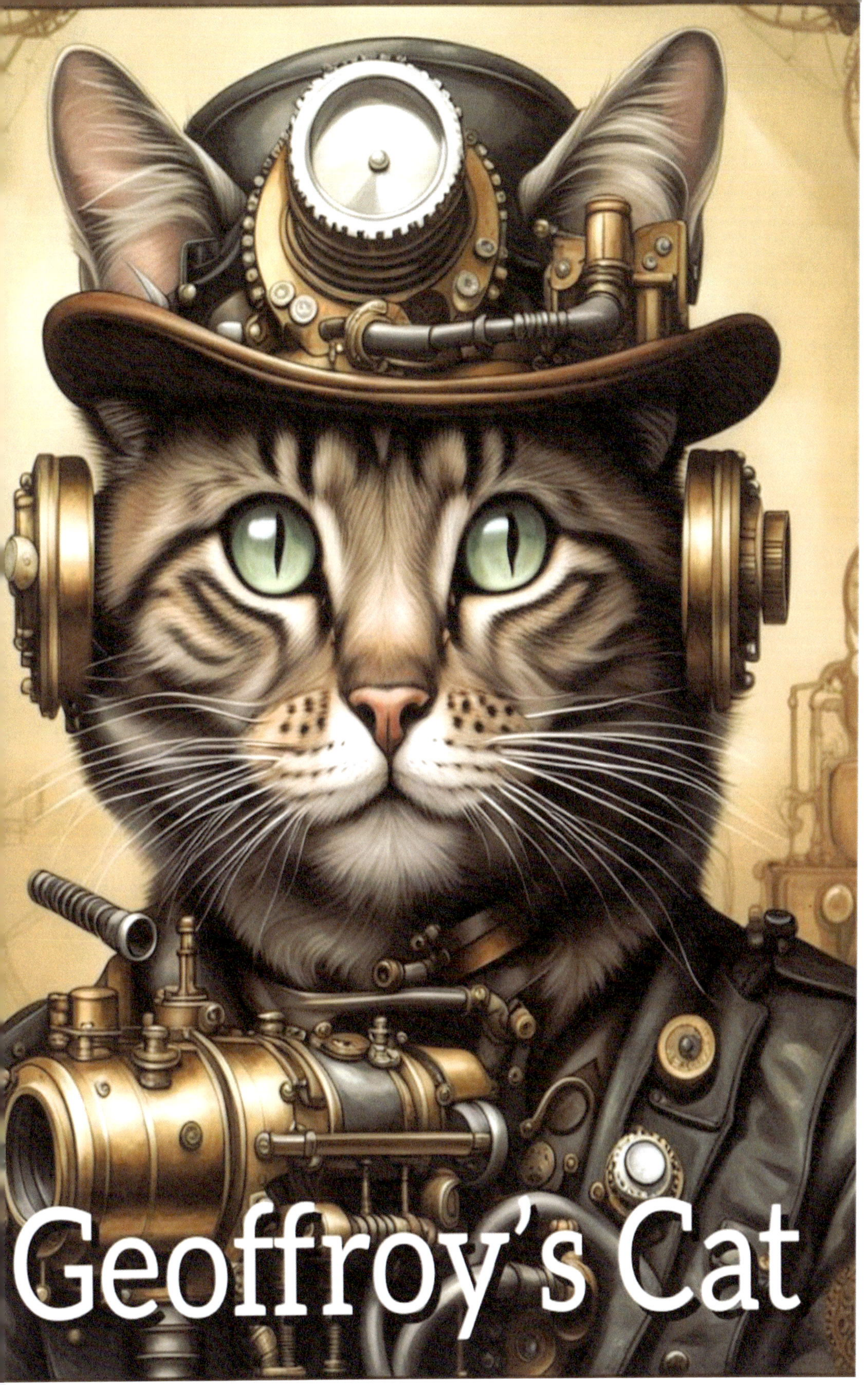
Geoffroy's Cat

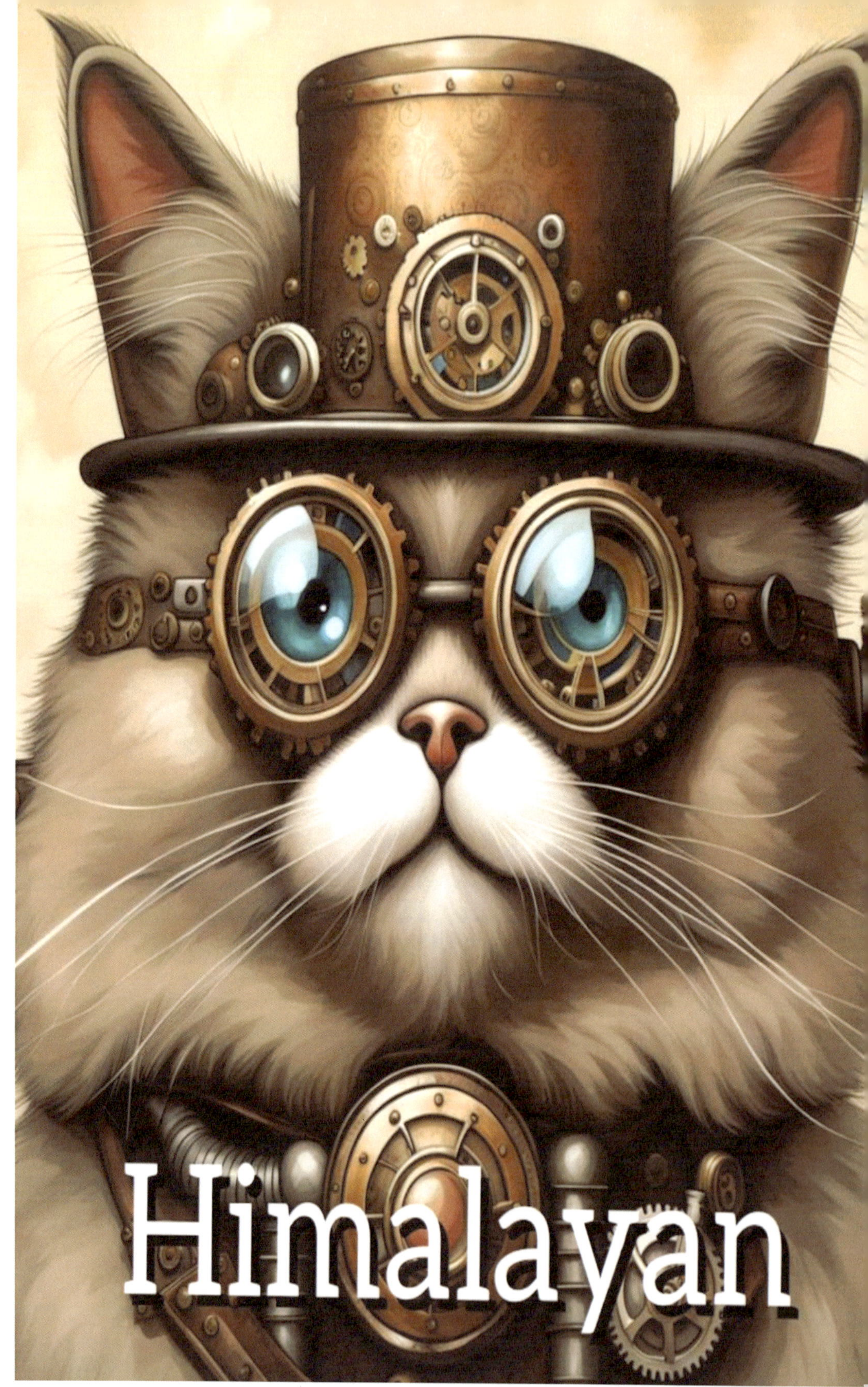
Himalayan

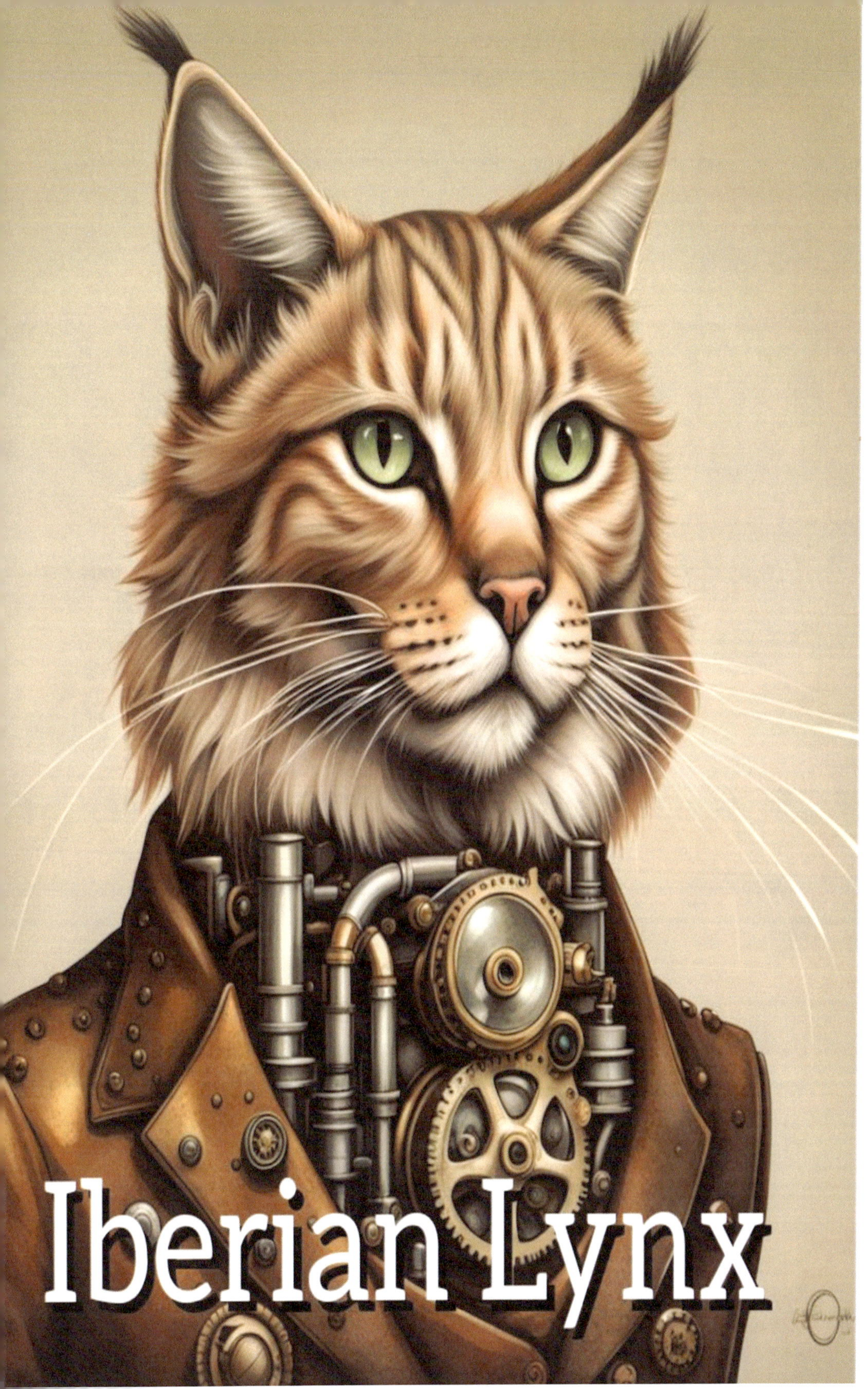
Iberian Lynx

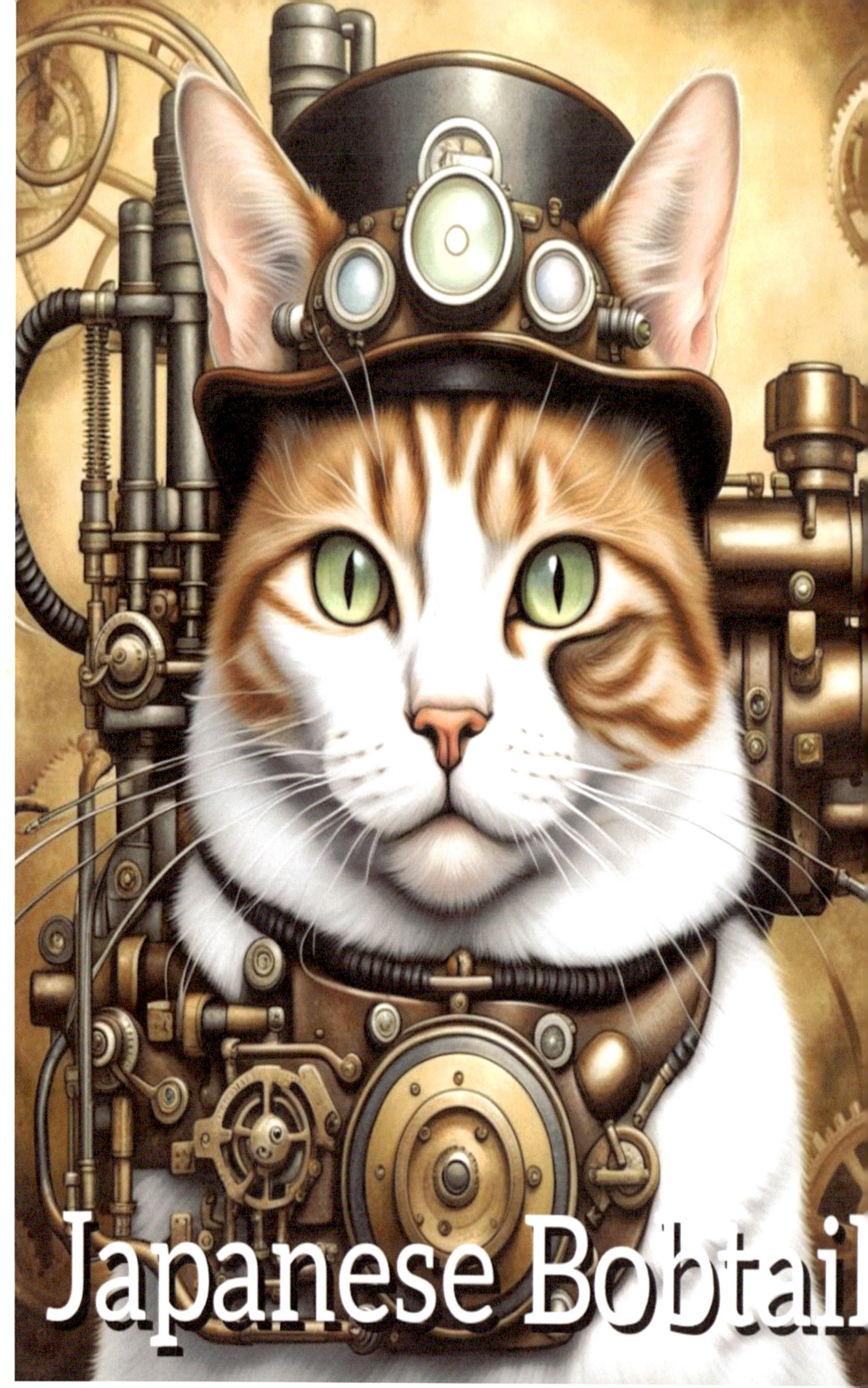

Japanese Bobtail

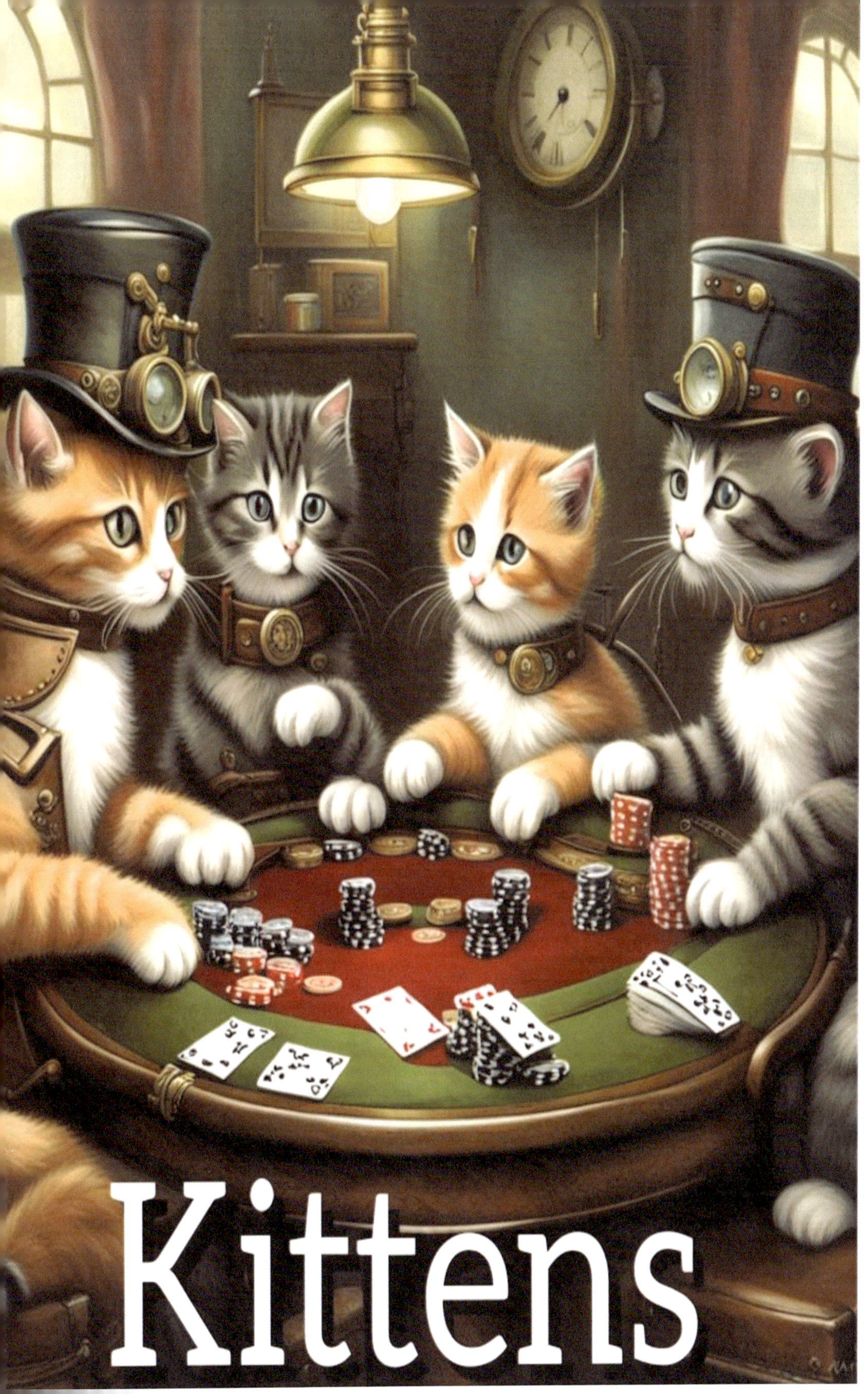

Kittens

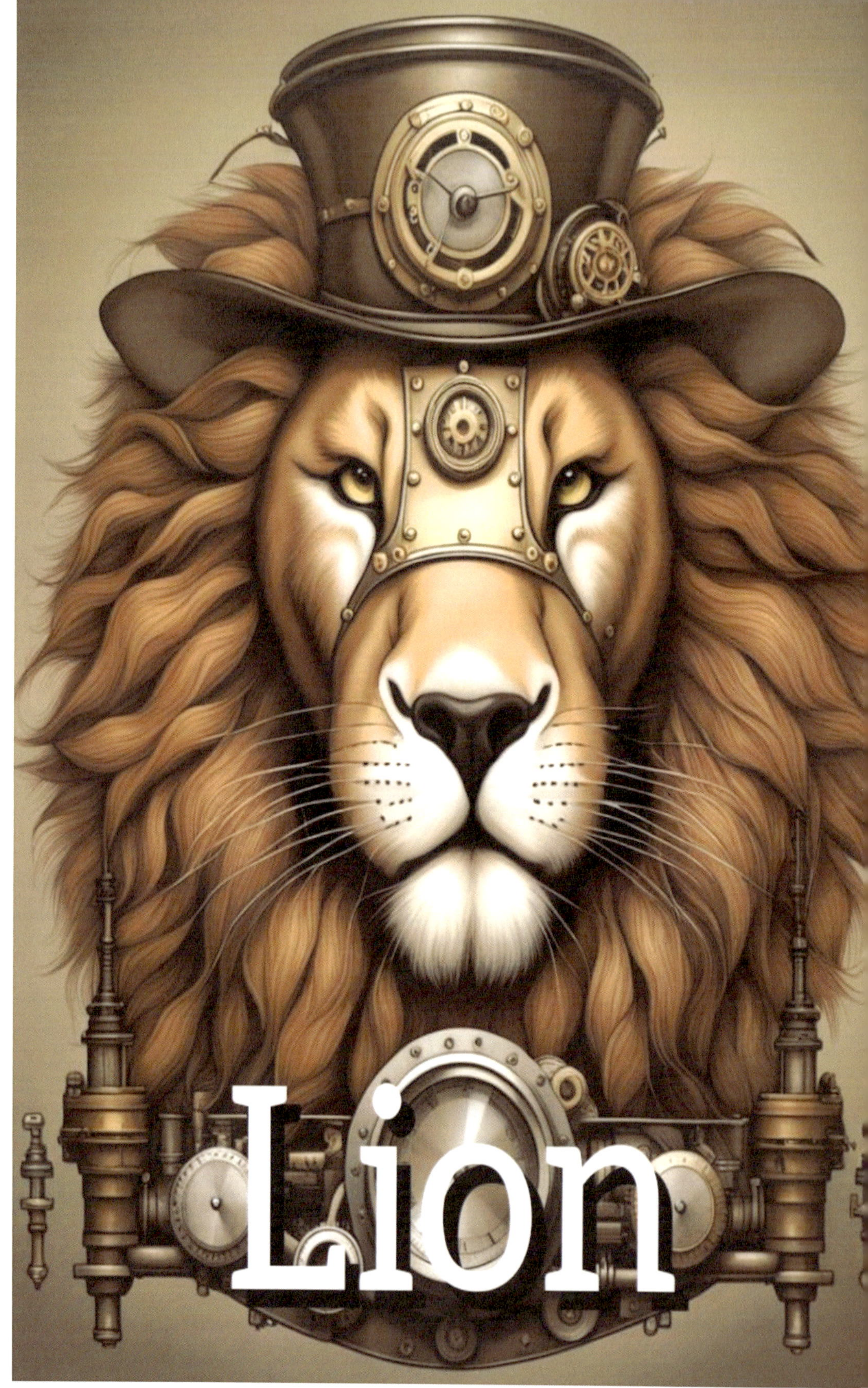
Lion

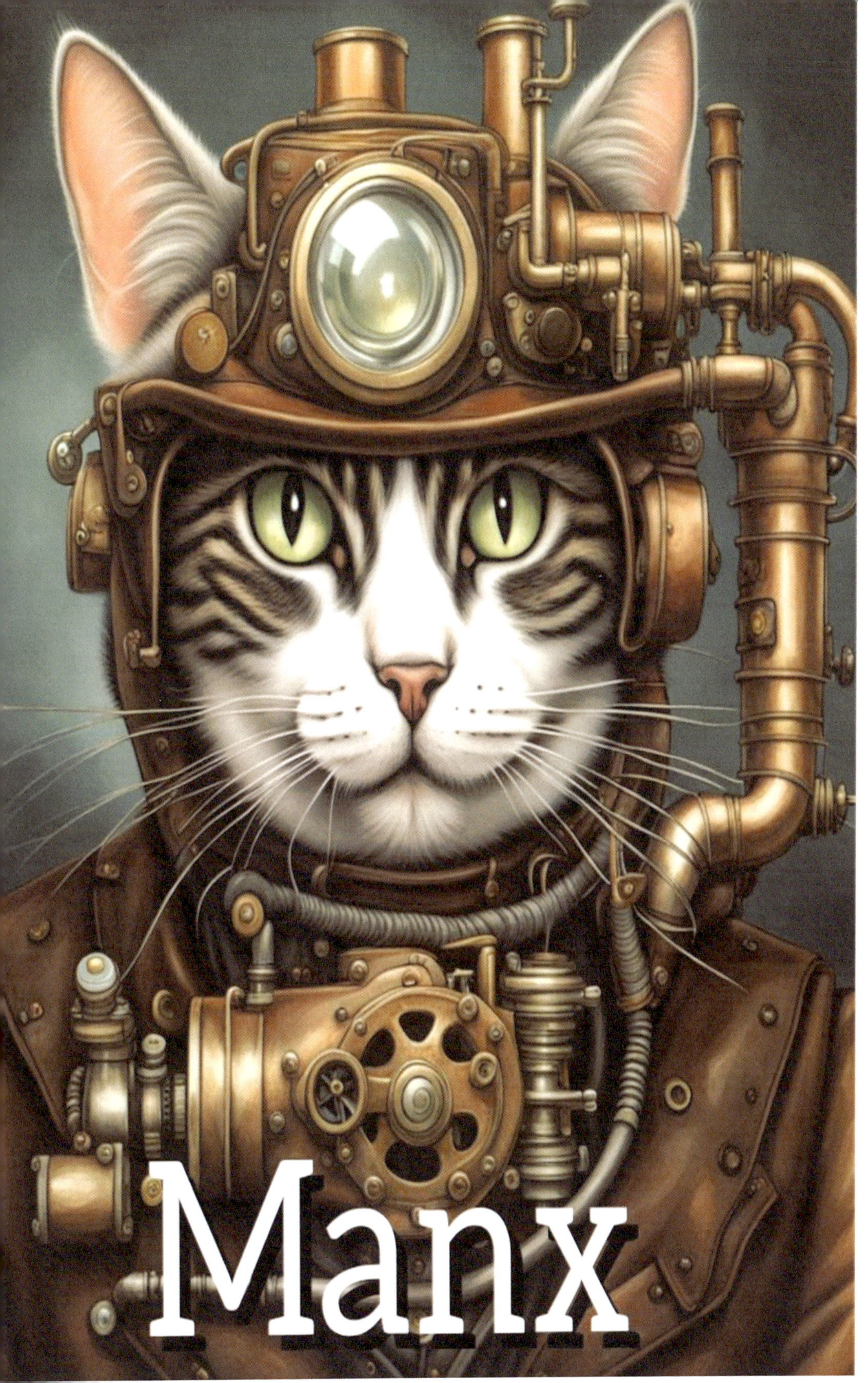
Manx

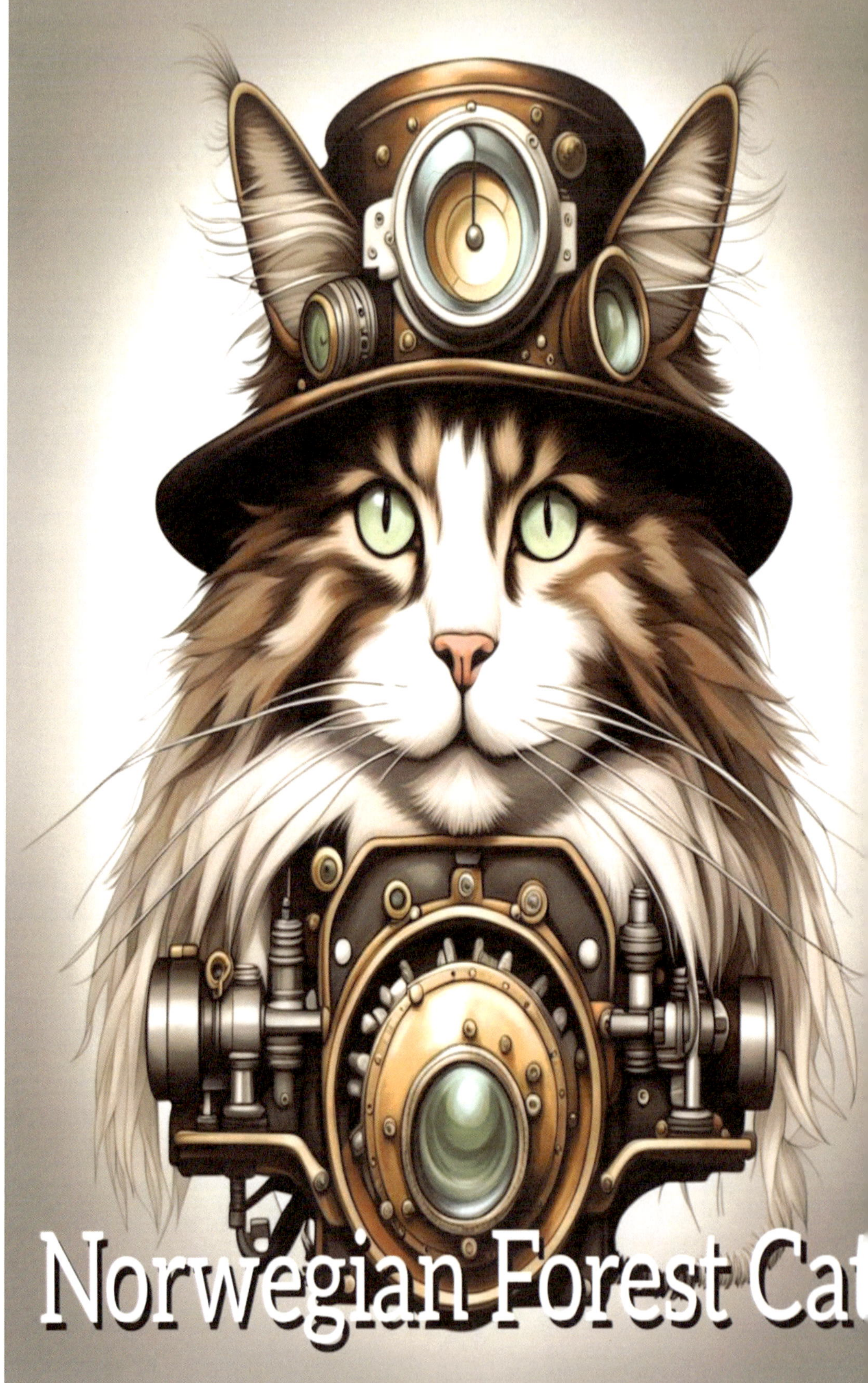
Norwegian Forest Cat

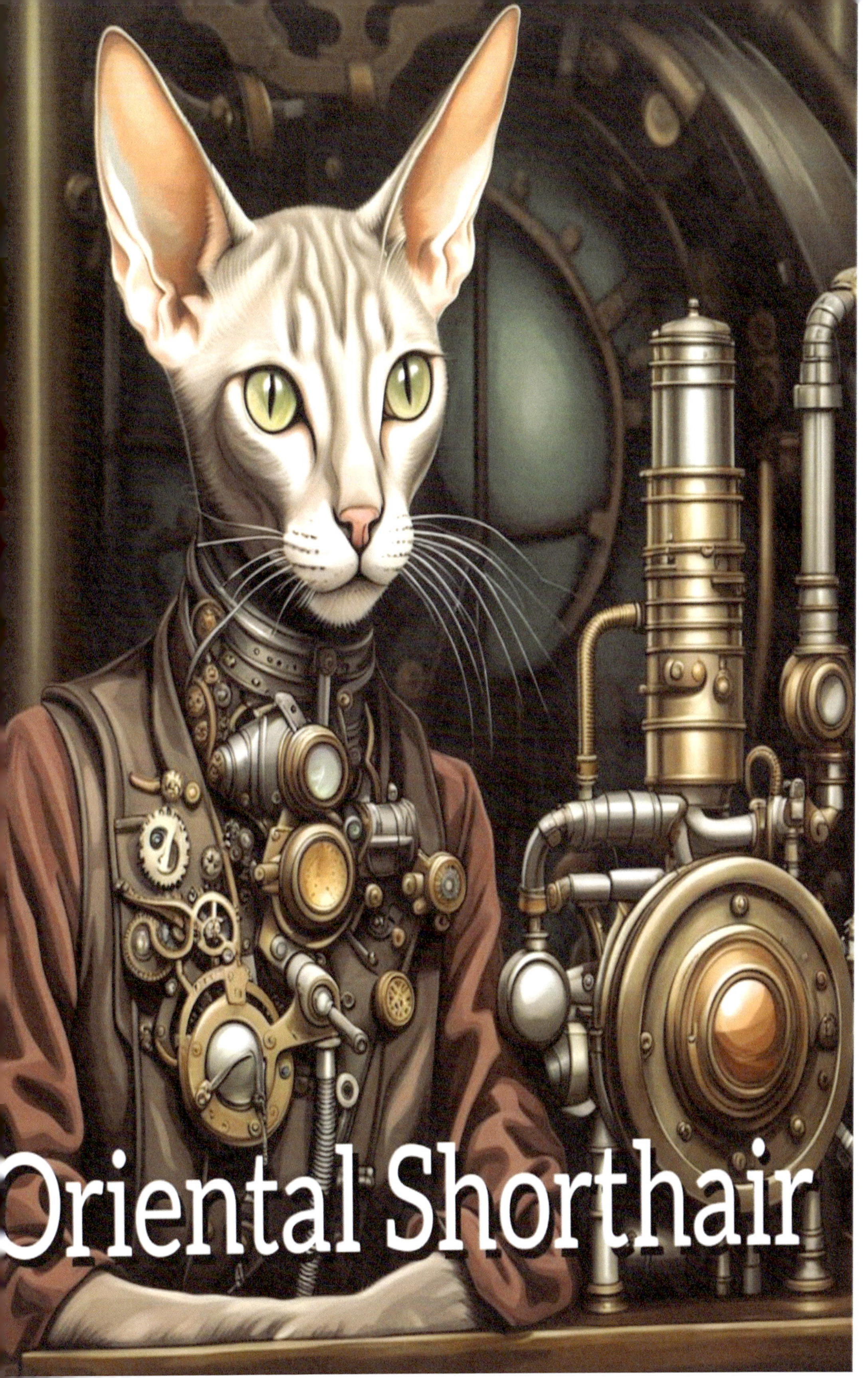
Oriental Shorthair

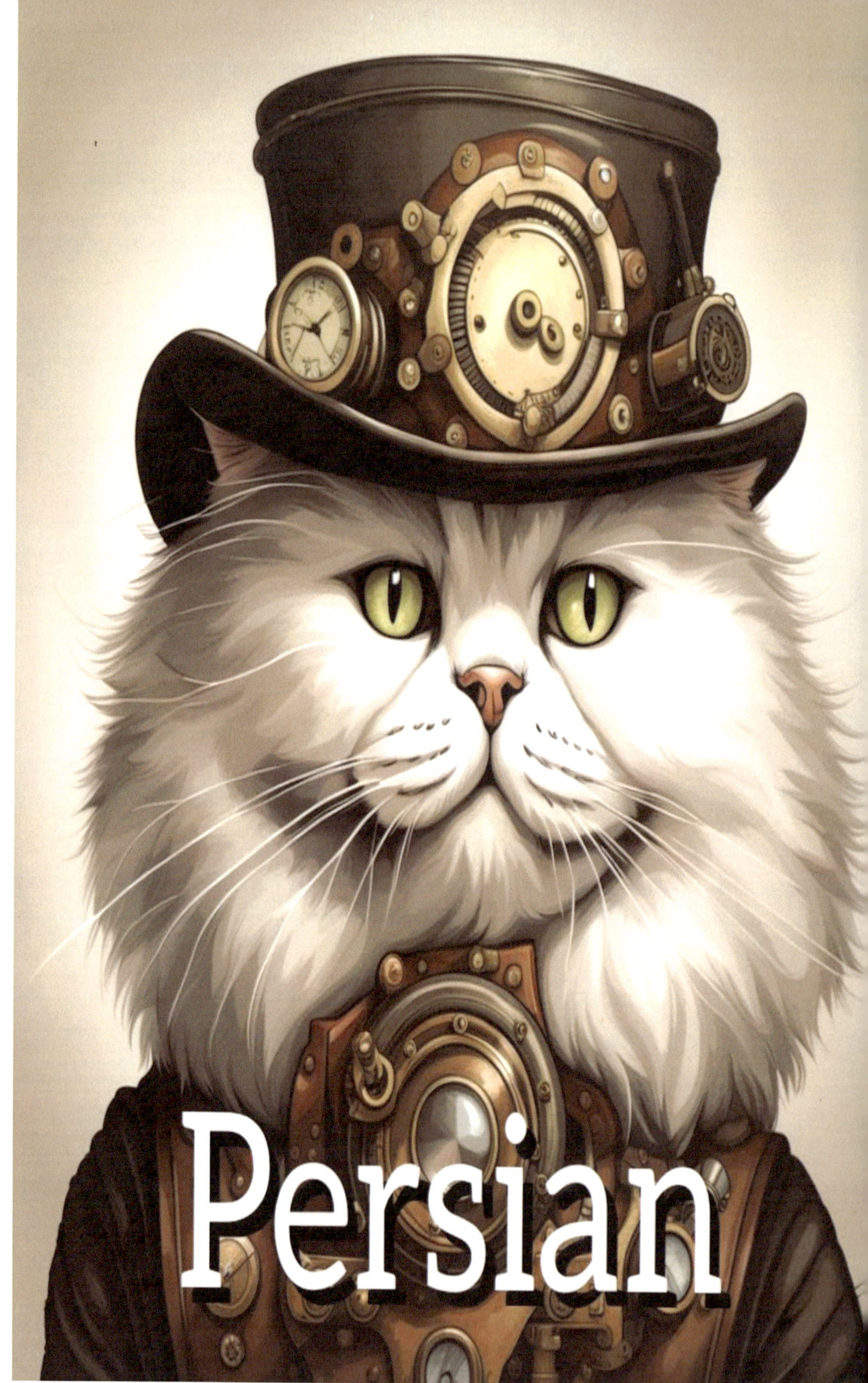
Persian

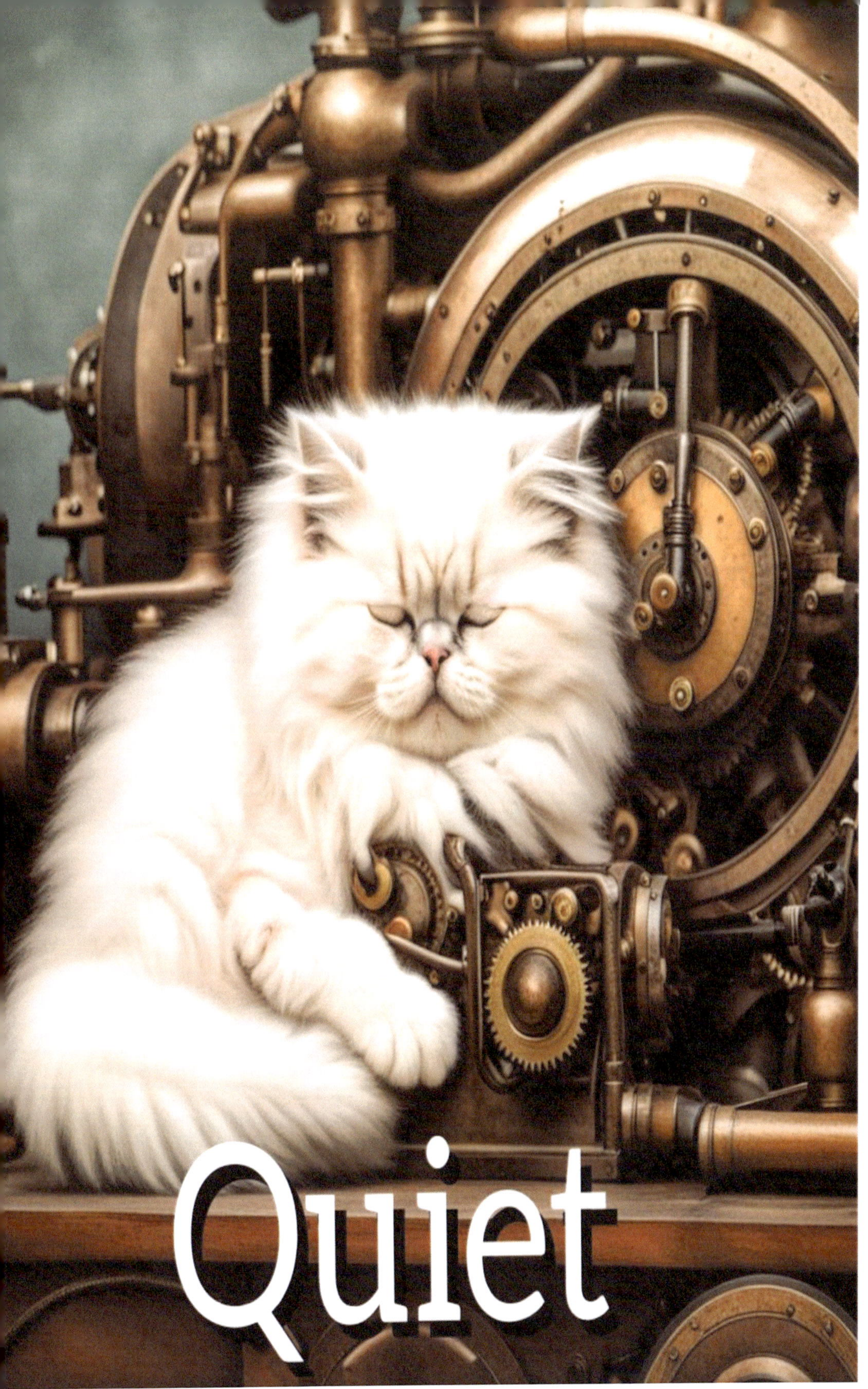
Quiet

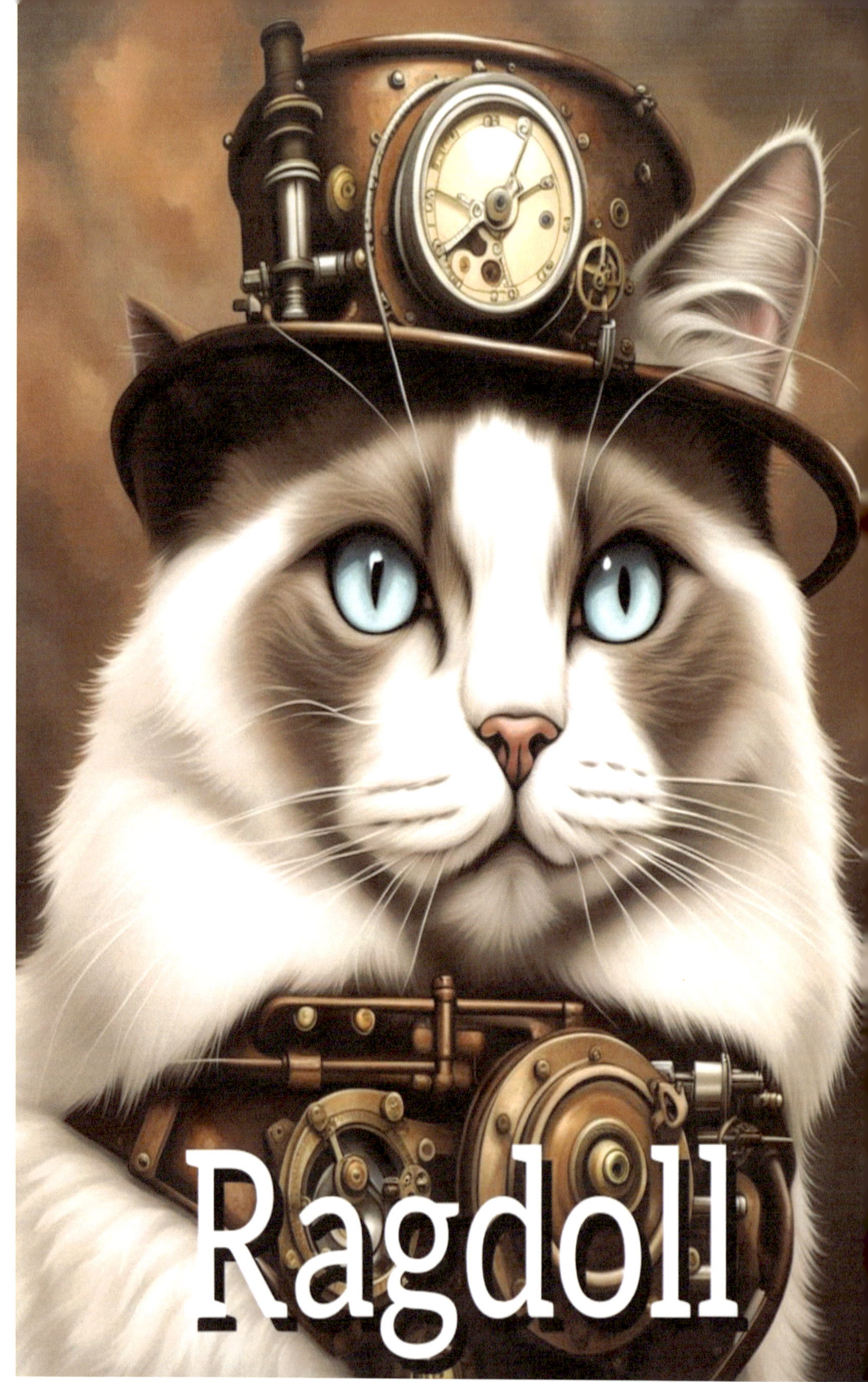
Ragdoll

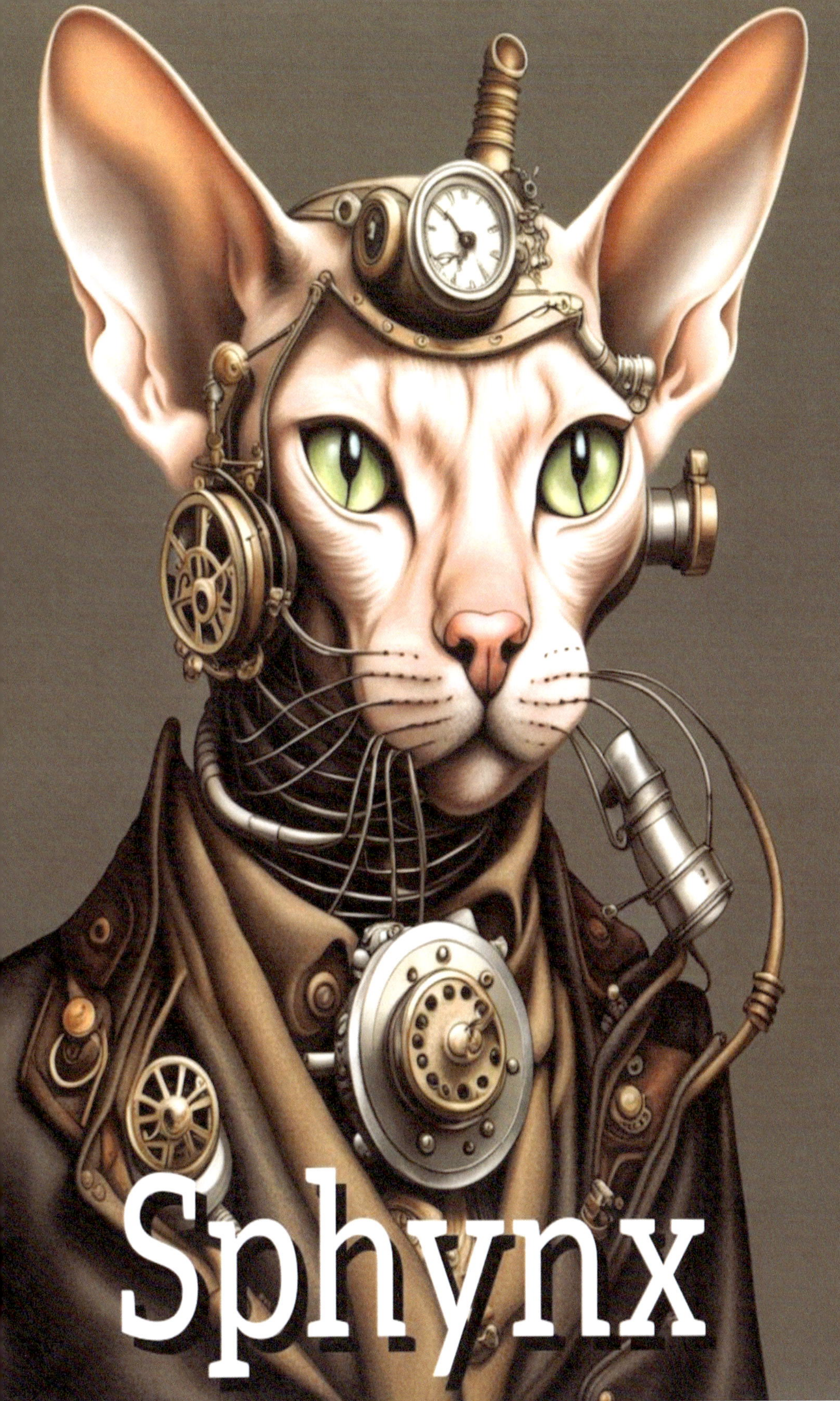

Sphynx

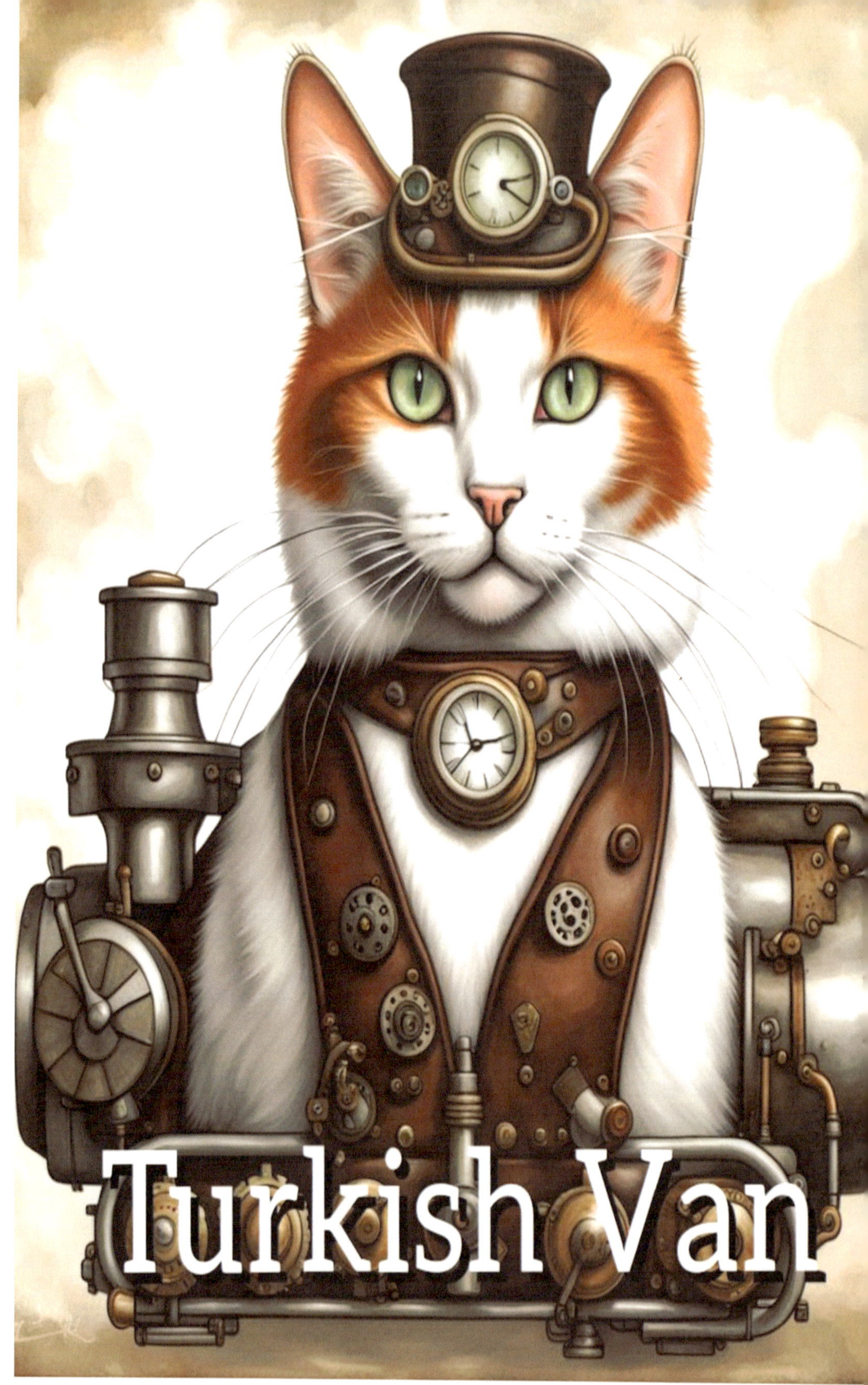
Turkish Van

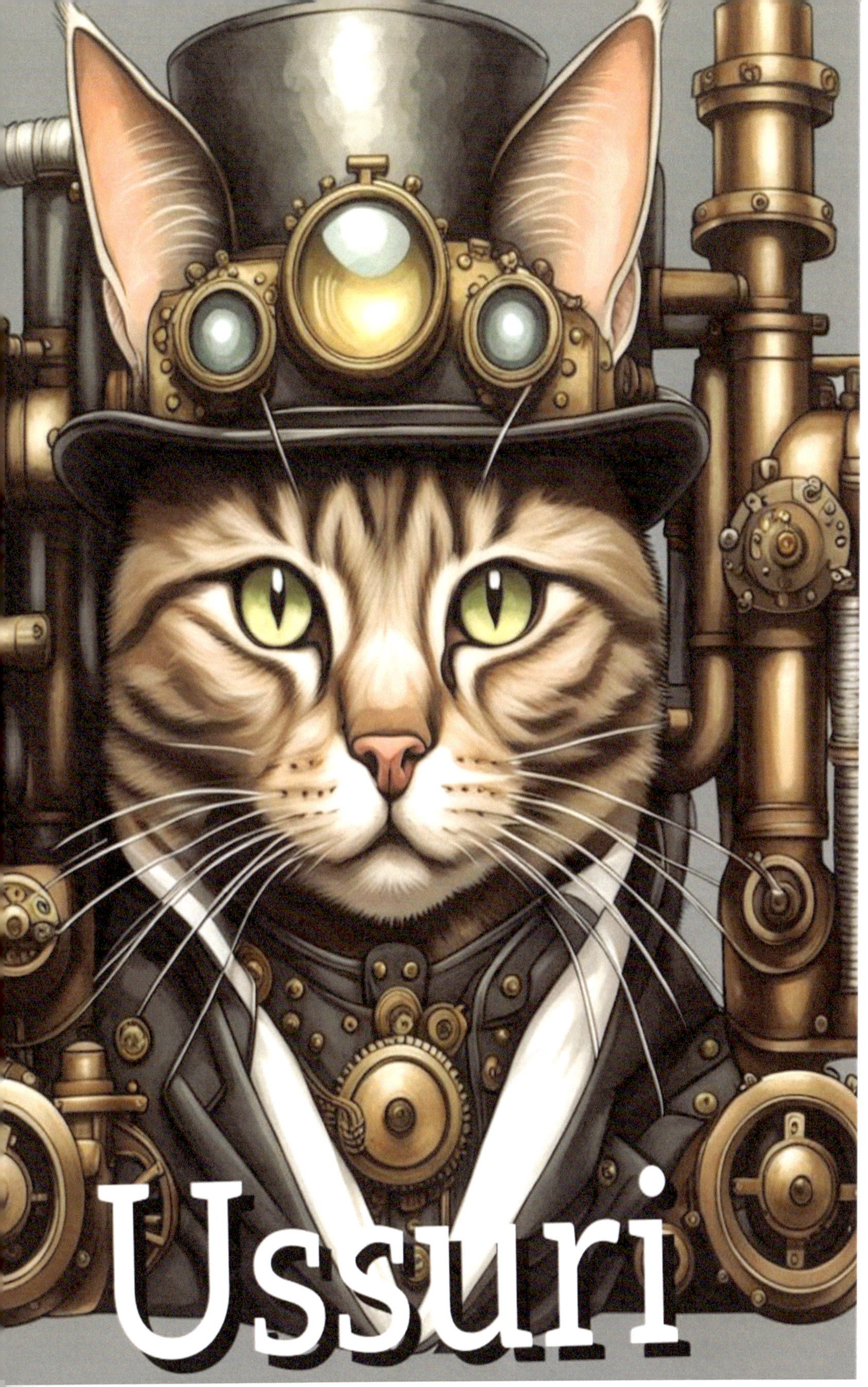
Ussuri

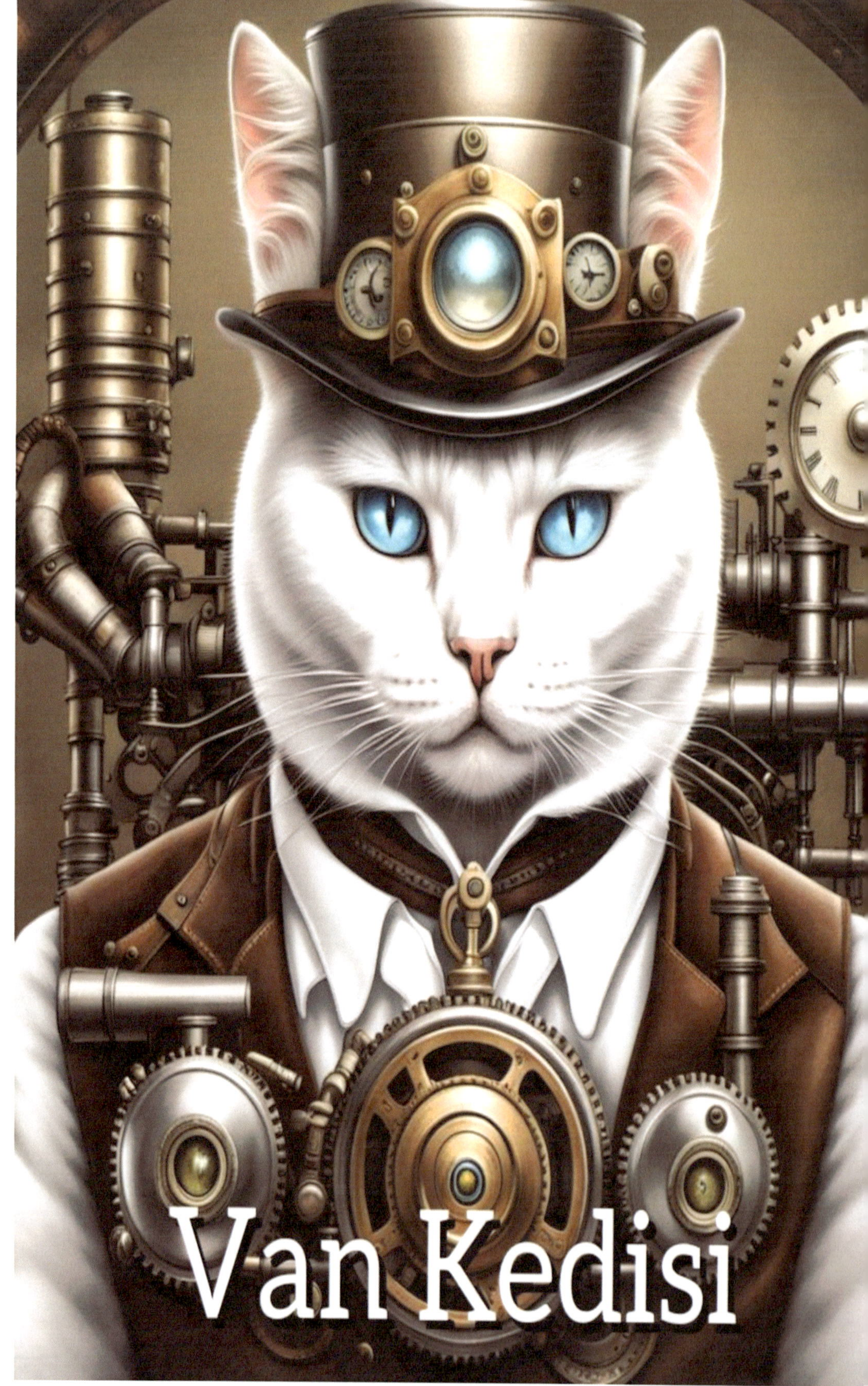
Van Kedisi

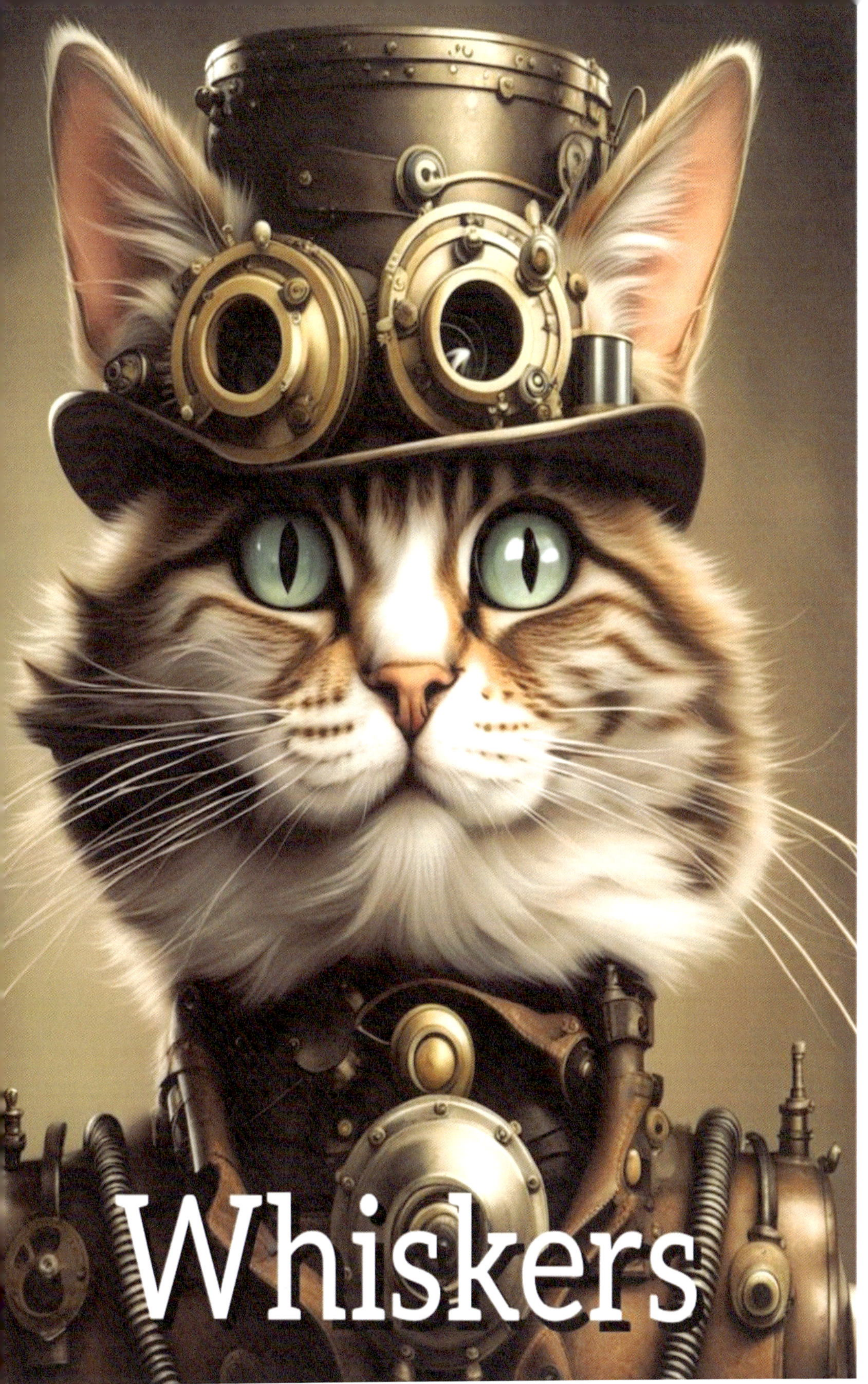
Whiskers

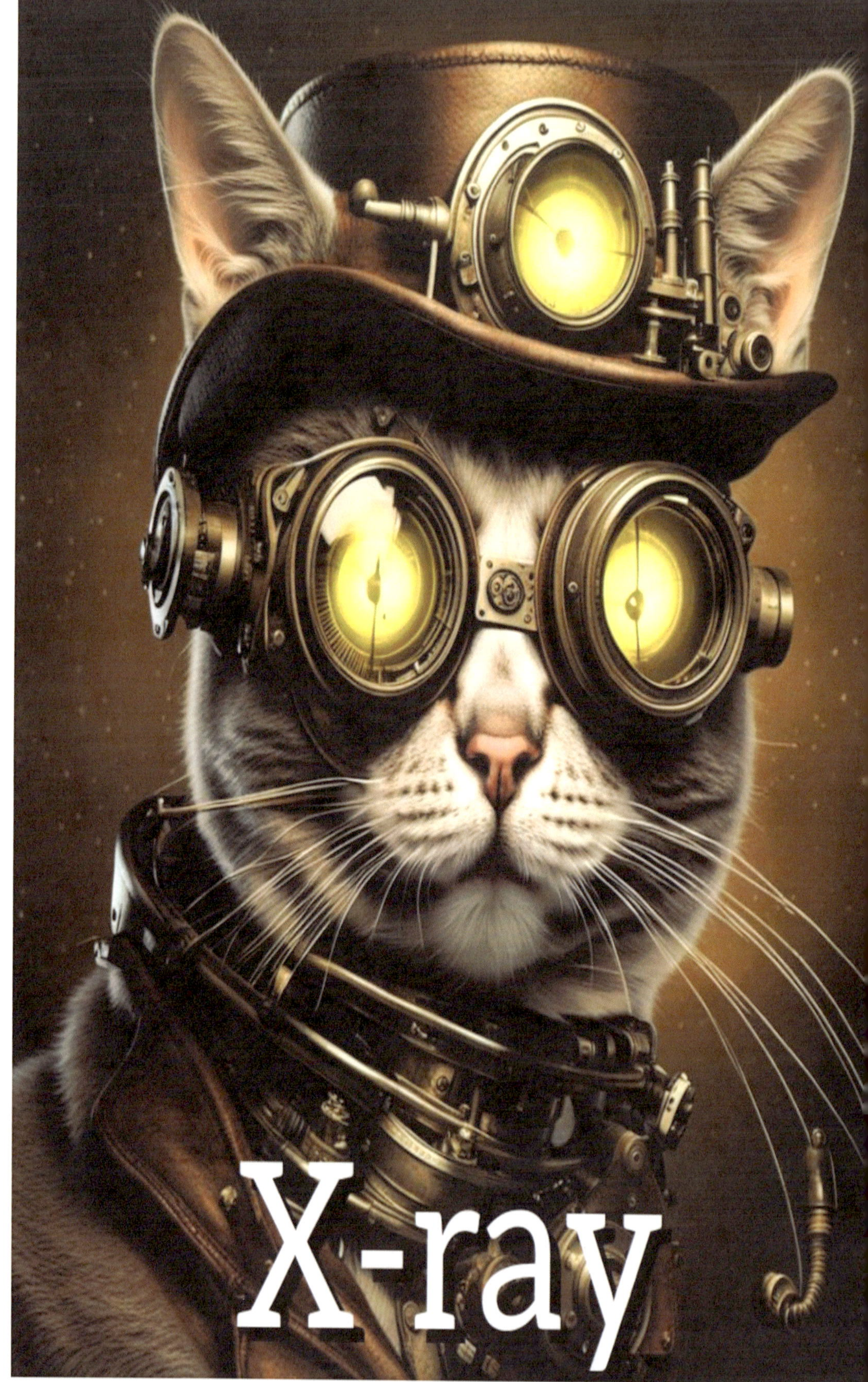

X-ray

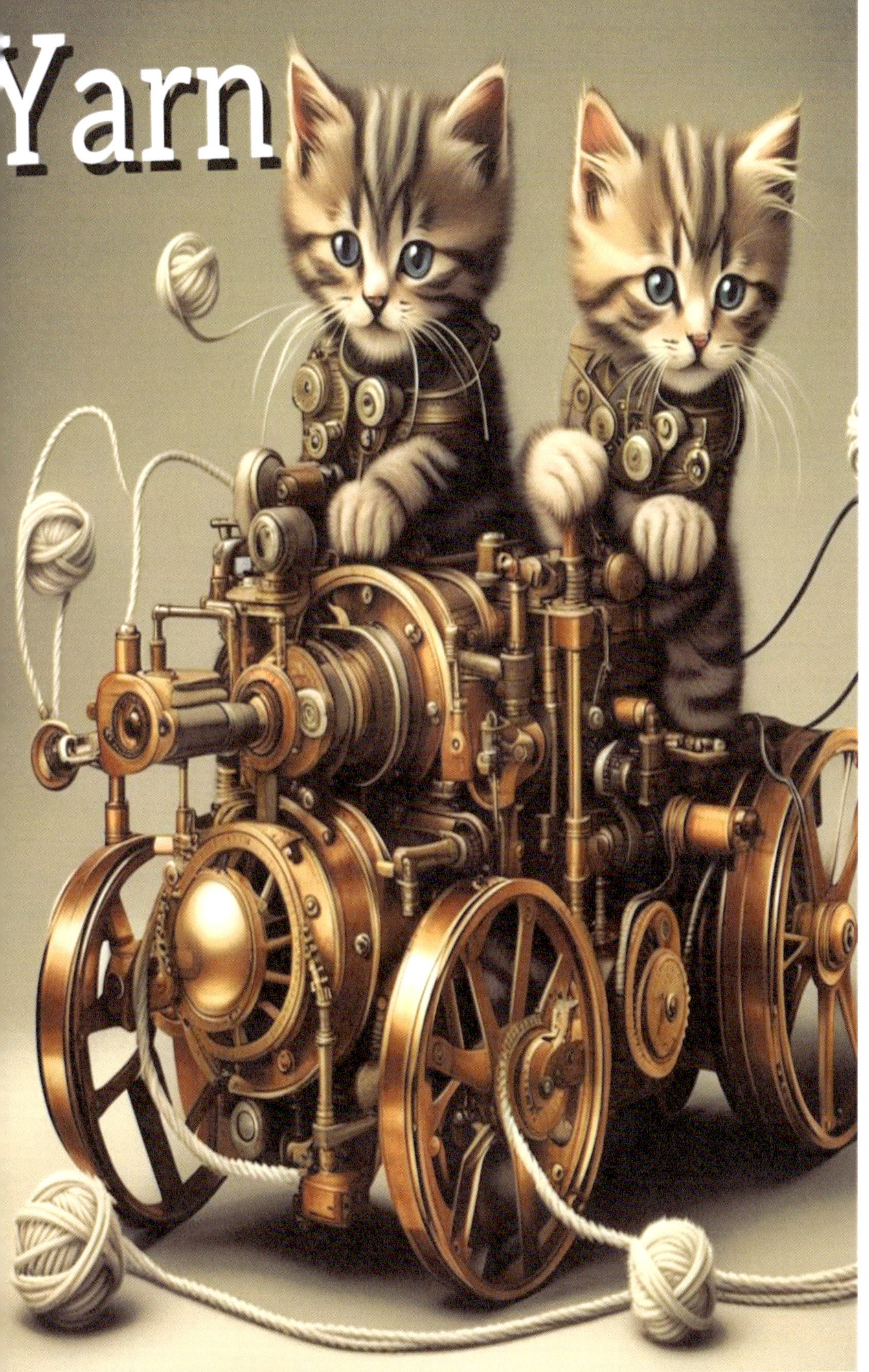
Yarn

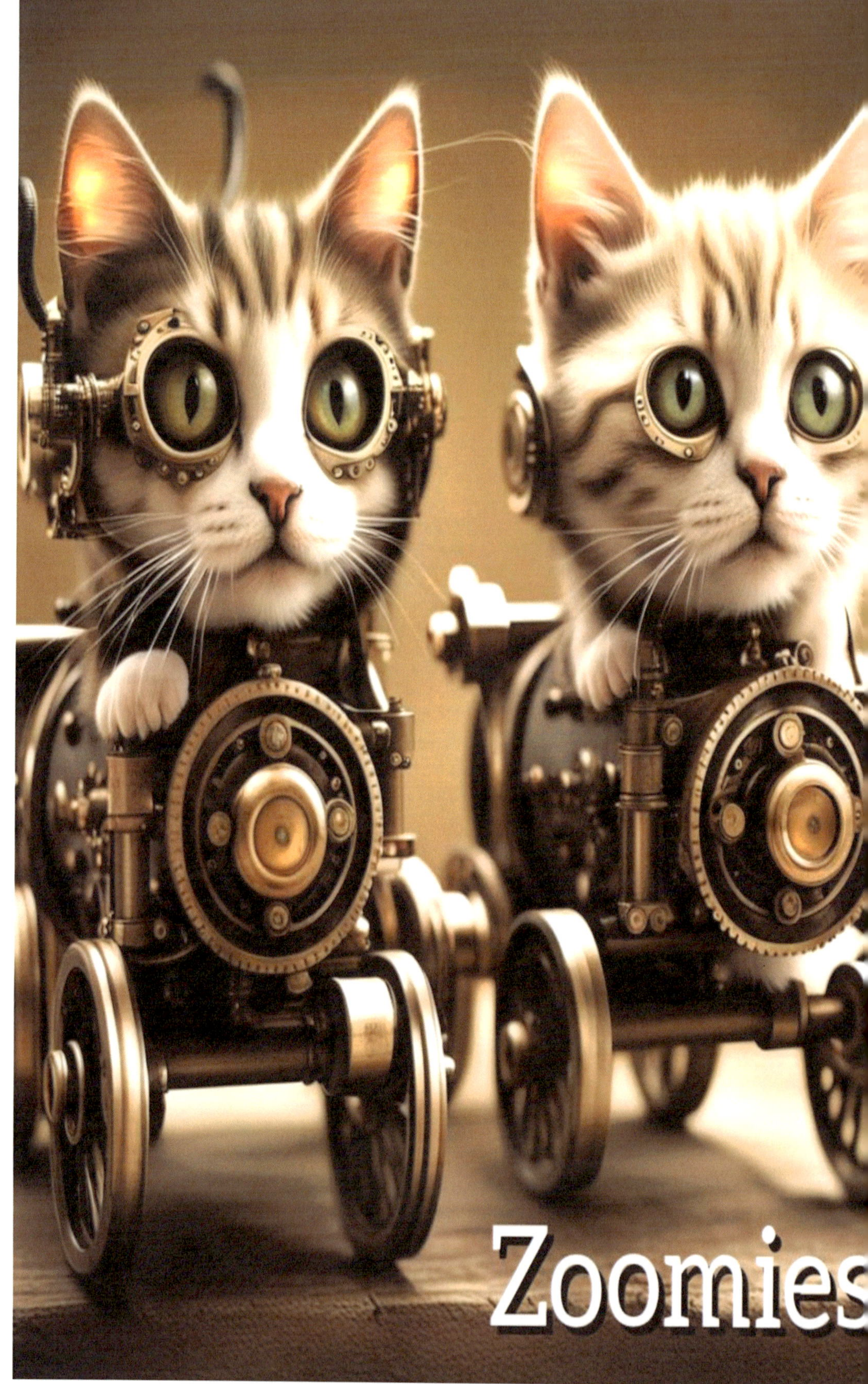
Zoomies